We're friends for Keeps

Written by Danielle Leduc McQueen

Illustrated by Claudia Guariglia

Among a lifetime of friends,

there are those rare friends.

The friends who stick with you,
who really know you,

who grow and change with you
but somehow stay exactly the same.

The friends you wouldn't trade
for a trip into outer space.

You and me?
We're those friends.

We're friends for Keeps.

Being friends for keeps
is like listening
to a playlist of the
best summer songs
on repeat, forever.

It's the shared
memories of
a soundtrack
only we know.

Friends for Keeps
is long chats and
endless heart-to-hearts.

It's a dresser full
of borrowed clothes,
and a thousand
frame-worthy photos.

Friends for Keeps means
never going more than a
few days without talking.

It's texting each other
when we're in the same room
(on the same couch).

You and me?

We can tell a whole story
in a single emoji.

We can turn empty
hours into adventures,
and quiet nights into
two-person parties.

Being friends for keeps is never-ending inside jokes. It's little secrets and a way of communicating that's **all our own.**

Friends for keeps means going weeks or months without seeing each other and having nothing change at all.

Except our hairstyles.

We share it all—
the insecurities, the judgments,
and the dark, hidden bits of
ourselves that don't normally
see the light of day.

We take risks together,
   make mistakes together, and
recover together (with pizza),
   just you and me.

No romance could derail us.
No move could tear us apart.
No drama will ever get in our way.

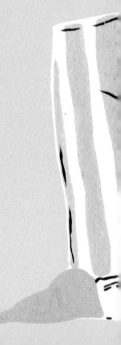

We'll outlast anything,
because we understand each other—
one hundred percent.

You and me?

We're as close
as it gets.

We've never laughed harder
than with each other.
We're even better together
than we are on our own.

When you have this much history with someone, and this many incredible stories, you're connected for Keeps.

Friends for keeps
is no small talk.

It's do or die.
    It's all or nothing.

And we've got it all.

We have a friendship
to last until we're
wrinkled and gray
(and then some).

Which is to say...

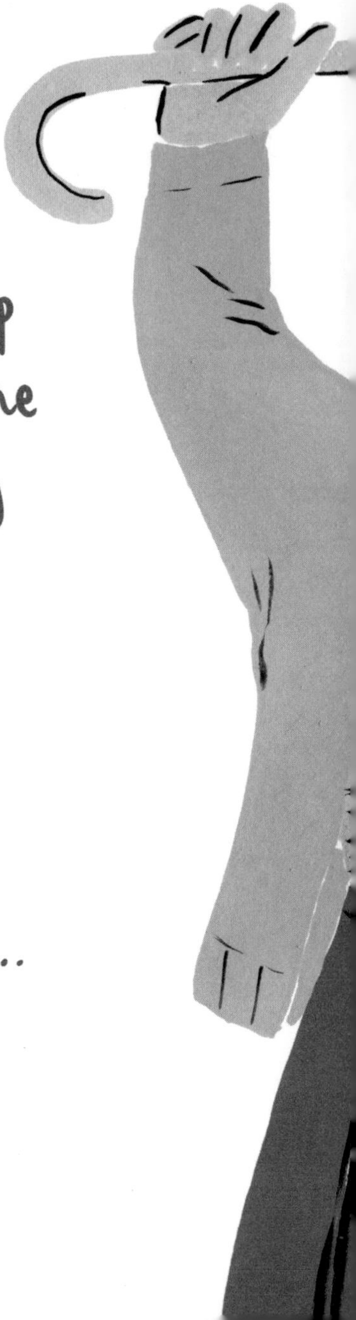

I love you for keeps,

my beautiful, amazing friend.

COMPENDIUM®
live inspired

Written by: Danielle Leduc McQueen

Illustrated by: Claudia Guariglia

Edited by: Ruth Austin

Designed and Art Directed by: Justine Edge

Library of Congress Control Number: 2019957947 | ISBN: 978-1-970147-21-6

1st printing. Printed in China with soy inks on FSC®-Mix certified paper.

*Create
meaningful
moments
with gifts
that inspire.*

CONNECT WITH US
live-inspired.com | sayhello@compendiuminc.com

     @compendiumliveinspired
#compendiumliveinspired